The Hidden Canyon

The Hidden

John Blaustein

A Studio Book

glitter with the dawn-light of Creation, it seems almost funny to worry about what we do to it. The proud dams above and below, those ugly concrete plugs Ed Abbey would like to blow up, are at worst fleeting aberrations. And though there is much concern over what we may be instigating in the Canyon by traveling through it on rafts and in boats, there seems to be widespread agreement that we are scarcely leaving enough twentieth-century artifacts and drowned corpses behind to provide a decent fossil record of our times in the siltstone forming under Lake Mead.

If for nothing more than the enjoyment, instruction, and inspiration of the transitory race called human, we should be determined to sustain the river experience in the Grand Canyon. Few things in this world are really beyond description, but it is safe to say that the exhilaration attendant upon entering and running a big Grand Canyon rapid in a small boat is one of them. Add to the scores of rapids the compelling subjects for contemplation (including, at times, the responses of your fellow wayfarers, and yes, even the sandstorms, rainstorms, and the inevitable cuts and bruises) and there is nothing more, with the possible exception of a hot shower now and again, that anyone should ask of life.

The rules and regulations governing activities along the canyon rims and down the trails have more than kept pace with the growth of traffic on the river. If you view them as incontrovertible law, it is now illegal to do quite a few things traditionally done on wilderness outings by normal folks. Aside from the prohibition against doffing your life jacket even if the nearest riffle is five miles away, the ordinances are in recognition of the worsening (from the human point of view) scarcity of camping space along the river as the daily surge from the power plant of Glen Canyon Dam scoops away at what is left of the beaches. Someone else will come along, looking for a good place to bed down, within a few days after you vacate your camp. So you don't build a fire that will leave soot on the ground, or throw out the dishwater, or go to the toilet where there is no toilet, unless you are a long way from the river. These constraints are matters of courtesy as well as regulation, so that there will be as little evidence as possible of your passage to offend later visitors. But also, out of respect for the more or less defenseless forms of native life, you don't walk in small streams or shampoo your hair in them, and you step aside for bumblebees, tarantulas, and snakes.

· · ·

The first time I saw Edward Abbey he was not yet famous, so it must have been eight or nine years ago. Our party was at Lee's Ferry, readying our beautiful Grand Canyon Dories for a three-week trip. In those gentler, less pressured times we had not yet been ordered down to the hot gravel flat where the big motorized baloney boats were inflated and rigged for launching. Our mooring lines ran up through the horsetail and grasses into the shade of an old willow tree where Abbey, having mentioned that the reason he was wearing a National Park Service shirt was that he was a combination truck driver and substitute ranger there to inspect our put-in, sat drinking a can of our beer. It was not until I saw his picture on the jacket of *Desert Solitaire*, long enough afterward for him to have grown a beard and to have gotten into print, that I remembered the name on the nameplate under the big easy grin back there on the riverbank.

After *Desert Solitaire*, the embarrassed Interior Department (they embarrass readily, as well they should) tried to keep Abbey out of sight. No fire-lookout tower was too remote to be his assigned station; I imagine that before he parted company with the Park Service he had many a quiet hour with little to do but put rebellious publishable things on paper at government expense.

He loves to shock, and does it well in writing, although he just can't bring it off in person. With letdown or relief, or more often both, we one day run up against this iconoclast, this rebel with cause, this terrorist of the typewriter, this Bolshevik with lighted fuses sputtering from every pocket and even from his inside-out cowboy boots, and we find him the gentlest of men, seeming unsure of himself in human company, and always the soul of conservatism.

Edward Abbey is hardly alone in his protest. In their way, the dories are elements of *our* protest, but by no means all of it. For the next eighteen days, three of the seven dories—the *Tapestry Wall*, the *Moqui Steps*, and the *Music Temple*—will keep reminding Abbey of the hateful dam that motivated *The Monkey Wrench Gang* after burying these wonders of Glen Canyon under the water of "Lake" Powell.

.   .   .

Incredibly, everything is stowed—all the things we need plus the things the government says we need. Author Abbey, unaccustomed to being guided and cared for by others, looks a bit self-conscious as he perches, in a bright new life vest, beside his lovely bride Renée in the *Peace River*, but he will get over that as the canyon days unfold. This is a scheduled public trip in which the twenty-two participants ("passengers" does not seem quite right, somehow) are of ages twelve through seventy-seven, from all walks of life, as they say, and from all over the country and one or two foreign countries to boot. For the next seventeen nights they will sleep on the ground, and in the days between they will drift through gorges no artist could ever depict and crash through cataracts no open-water sailor would ever believe. When they feel like it, they will explore ashore, up the side canyons to secret springs and gardens and to the ancient buildings where vanished races dwelt a thousand years ago. They will watch the bighorn's leaping ascent of the cliffs, the eagle's soaring flight along the rimrock. They will get to know the beavers, ravens, ouzels, wood rats, lizards, and cacomistles that have never learned to fear humans because they have never had to. They will see the horrors wrought upon the Canyon by the Bureau of Reclamation's test diggings at Mile 39 ("Marble damsite") and by the National Park Service's channelization of Bright Angel Creek into a riprapped storm drain at Mile 88. And occasionally they will meet other parties, most of them traveling by baloney boat.

One of our oarsmen-guides is John Blaustein. Years have been speeding by, and it's hard to keep in mind that John was only twenty-two when he wangled his way into our outfit as cook's helper. When he did get a boat on his second trip, I had to keep admonishing him to stop telling the passengers how frightened he was every time he approached a rapid. A shade too clean looking to fit the image of a river guide, he was a bit slow in gaining acceptance, but when it did come it was complete, and he now ranks at the top, not only for handling a spirited dory in whitewater but also as a host and guide.

I don't know when John Blaustein decided to become a photographer, but his artistry with a camera does not need to be proved by listing his honors here. All you have to do is turn the page.

Martin Litton

and the shade of the canyon walls, we are all mighty glad to see Wally's boat pulled ashore on the beach above the mouth of North Canyon. Twenty miles from Lee's Ferry and our second camp. Eight miles yesterday, twelve today. Too fast to suit some of us but better than most do. (The motorized pontoon rafts average thirty to forty miles per day.)

Unloading the dories has become part of a welcome routine. Most of the passengers help out, and scrounge for firewood and carry water. My wife Renée, the tall, slim girl with the legs, has already made herself an integral member of the kitchen crew. Only a few more sensitive types like myself, pained by the sight of toil and turmoil, sneak away for a walk up North Canyon.

You can walk for only a mile or so till you come to an impassable waterfall—dry now—fifty feet high. Below is a small clear pool, evaporating. The silence here, away from the river and the people, is intense. The clash of stone against stone, in the dry air, is harsh, brittle, without resonance or echo. A silence almost supernatural that reminds me of the oppressive stillness in the final scenes of Kubrick's *2001*. I can hear the blood singing in my ears. The sky above, beyond the crooked canyon rim, is a pale metallic blue. Storm coming.

That evening the wind begins to blow. Dark clouds loom, and lightning crackles in the distance. Will it rain? Wally studies the sky. "I can say," he says, "without doubt or qualification, that it might. If not here, somewhere." Renée and I string up our plastic tube tent, supplied by Litton's Dories, Inc., tying one end to a dead arrowweed and the other to a snake. "Hobble that snake." Well, a stick. There's nothing else available. It doesn't rain but all night long the wind howls and the sand swirls in our faces.

DAY 3 Today is a good day. John lets me row his boat. We easily navigate past 24½ Mile Rapid, where Bert Loper, the "Grand Old Man of the Colorado," died in 1949, while rowing himself down the river in celebration of his eightieth birthday. John lets me take the dory through 29 Mile Rapid, rated 4, and the riffle at Mile 30. All goes well at 29 Mile, but at the riffle I barely get around the exposed rock at the head of the chute and am forced to "Powell" the rest of it, stern foremost. Backwards. Like Powell did it. The dory does equally well in either attitude but John is obviously shaken. "Exciting," he says, his knuckles white, "very exciting. Give me back the oars, please."

I thought it was a good run. Any run without loss of boat or passengers is a good run, in my opinion. We pause at Vasey's Paradise for a drink of clear spring water.

August 9, 1869—The river turns sharply to the east and seems enclosed by a wall set with a million brilliant gems. On coming nearer we find fountains bursting from the rock high overhead and the spray in the sunshine forms the gems which bedeck the wall. The rocks are covered with mosses and ferns and many beautiful flowering plants. We name it Vasey's Paradise, in honor of the botanist who traveled with us last year.

Lunch at Redwall Cavern, Mile 33. Lemonade, beer, and avocado-cheese-bean-sprout sandwiches. Excellent. Redwall Cavern is a huge chamber carved out of the limestone by the old predamnation river. Major Powell guessed it would seat fifty thousand people. I'd say five thousand. He was off by a digit but assumed, when writing his celebrated report, that no one else would ever come down the river to check up on him. I'm not calling Powell a liar; Powell is a hero of mine.

But I will say he had a tendency, now and then, as a friend of mine says, to "overexaggerate."

The river, brown before, is taking on a rich red-orange color, *muy Colorado*. Lovely. The good old Paria must be in flood again. So that's where last night's storm was.

We run some modest rapids this afternoon, make third camp at Buck Farm Canyon, Mile 41, early in the evening. Much deer sign—thus the name?—and trickling seeps, emerald pools, tadpoles, red and blue and purple dragonflies, cottonwood, box elder, and the graceful little redbud trees. Back to camp. Soup and salad, steak and sweet corn, plenty of beer for supper. Happiness.

DAY 4 Off again on the river of gold, through a clear bright irreplaceable day. The great Redwall cliffs soaring above, intense and vivid against God's blue sky. Marble Canyon, Powell called this place, though limestone is not marble and he knew it.

At Mile 43, high on the right wall, maybe a thousand feet above the river, we see the remains of some kind of wooden footbridge joining one ledge to the next. Studied through binoculars, the wreckage appears old, very old, the work of Indians. What is it?

Where does it go? Is there a hidden Anasazi granary up there, a concealed pre-Columbian penthouse? I'd like to climb up and see where the bridge leads, if anywhere, but today we have no time for unscheduled stops, we pass on. Next time. I call it Mystery Footbridge in my notes.

We slip through President Harding Rapid (2–4). Onward. Sail on, sail on, oh jaunty dories and your pirate crew, with your cargo of living bodies, sunburned flesh, pothering brains.

We camp tonight at Nankoweap Canyon, Mile 52. The Bright Angel Shale is at river level here. "Nankoweap," Wally explains, "is an old Paiute word meaning 'Place where scorpions crawl into sleeping bags if not detected by unsleeping vigilance.'" Before dinner Renée and I hike up the talus slope under the cliffs to check out the ruins of Anasazi storage structures. Stones and dust; even the ghosts have long since departed.

DAY 5 Onward. We have come only fifty-two miles in four days. We have many miles, many rapids, many more rock formations to go, before this perilous journal is completed.

Kwagunt Rapid (4–6). No problem. 60 Mile Rapid (4). Simple. The Tapeats sandstone appears. We pass the mouth of the Little Colorado River, chocolate-brown with flood waters, and find new and formidable rock formations rising before us. Marble Canyon becomes the Grand Canyon itself. Powell recorded the approach in these words:

> *August 13, 1869—We are now ready to start on our way down the Great Unknown. We have but a month's rations remaining. We have an unknown distance yet to run, an unknown river to explore. With some eagerness and some anxiety and some misgiving we enter the canyon below. . . .*

Dramatic words. Melodramatic, perhaps. And yet with a little effort of the imagination we can understand how Powell and his brave men felt. For two months they'd been battling the river, all the way from Wyoming—upsetting in rapids, wrecking boats, losing supplies, gambling on Powell's belief that a river so silt-laden would not, as rumors had it, disappear underground or trap them between unscalable walls on the verge of a fatal waterfall. Now they were entering the biggest canyon yet, facing the worst rapids, without any sure knowledge of what lay ahead. And low on grub.

Above us on the right stands Chuar Butte. Still visible up there, far above the river, are the aluminum scraps of two big airliners that collided above the Grand Canyon in 1956: 128 went down; all died.

Tanner Rapid, Mile 69. Basalt Canyon, a volcanic region, with grim-looking blue-black cliffs set at a crazy angle to the descending river. We make camp above the roar of Unkar Rapid in the last broad open valley we shall see for the next two hundred miles. Not far downstream the river cuts into the pre-Cambrian gneiss and schists of the upper Granite Gorge, the inner canyon, where the big rapids make their play.

Half-moon in the sky tonight, casting a supernatural glow on the grotesque forms of the Canyon, on the wall known as Palisades of the Desert, on the remote promontory, thirty-five hundred feet above, of Cape Solitude. We can see the tree-lined South Rim, Desert View Tower, and, toward the north, Wotan's Throne.

Found a rattlesnake in the bush. A small one, three rattles, pinkish in color. He looked frightened. We left him alone.

DAY 6 A cool morning, overcast sky. More birds for Renée's list: brown-headed cowbird, western tanager, black-necked stilts, violet-green swallows, black-throated swifts. The swifts like to skim close to the waves in the rapids, attracted, it would seem, by the turbulent air. According to Rich Turner, one of our boatmen, they sometimes hit the waves and drown.

River rising but not high enough. Boatmen nervous about running the serious rapids with insufficient water. Those rocks, those granite fangs foaming with froth in the charging stream. Bad dreams.

We push onto a river the color of bronze, shimmering like hammered metal under the desert sun. Through Unkar—made it! Then 75 Mile Rapid (4–7). Still alive. We pull ashore above Hance Rapid (7–8) for study and consultation.

Hance is always a problem for the dorymen, especially in low water. Just too many goddamned rocks sticking up, or even worse, half-hidden near the surface. No clear route through. A zigzag course. Huge waves, treacherous boils, churning holes that can eat a boat alive. A kind of slalom for oarsmen, with the penalty for a mistake a possible smashed boat. The big advantage of rubber boats is that they can usually be bounced off the well-polished boulders in the rapids without suffering damage. Usually. But rigid crafts likes dories or kayaks may split, puncture, crack like an eggshell. Therefore

17

wave like a surfboard, is swallowed by the mouth, then instantly ejected, spat out, and shot downstream. The Eater rejects aluminum! Mike surfaces, swimming around the rocks and into the narrow channel on the right. His boat, miraculously upright and facing properly downriver, bow foremost, sails sedately through the Rock Garden without touching a rock. (Many a tale is told by boatmen, late at night when the passengers are asleep, of unmanned boats making their own way without harm or upset through the most horrendous of gnashing waterfalls.) Mike sees his boat coming, swims to it, climbs aboard. Only the oars are missing, but these are soon found and recovered (each dory carries two spares, just in case). Nobody ever ran Crystal that way before.

After Crystal we pass a series of side canyons with gemlike names: Agate, Sapphire, Turquoise, Ruby. Near Bass Rapid we see an old rusting metal boat stranded high on the left bank, far above the present waterline. Onward, through Shinumo Rapid, 110 Mile Rapid, Hakatai Rapid, and into Waltenberg (3–7). A sleeper. Waltenberg today reveals itself as a tough one—tremendous waves shutting out the sun. We plow through, Renée and I now riding in Mike's big boat. Mike's hands are sore, cut like his knees by rocks from his swim at Crystal. I row his heavy, leaky, water-laden boat the last two miles to our camp at Garnet Canyon. Twenty-one miles today—a record. We are wet, cold, tired, and murderously hungry. Kenly and Jane improvise a hasty dinner and we eat by the light of the waxing moon.

Later, resting on the sand, Mike lays his right hand on a rock and gets stung by a scorpion. A Giant Hairy Desert scorpion, which escapes. Mike doses himself with cortisone and spends a long night hallucinating, aided by the moon, by the stone gargoyles on the canyon rim, and by the image of the Eater gaping wide beneath his dory. Mike's turn; we all have days like that.

DAY 8 In the morning Mike's hand is swollen badly. I row the boat for him from Garnet to Elves Chasm, Mile 116, and from there to our next camp above Blacktail Canyon at the head of Conquistador Aisle, a straight stretch of river three miles long, rare in the otherwise continual turns and twists of the Colorado.

We spend much of the day at Elves Chasm, a magical place with running stream, clear pools, high falls, lush and varied vegetation. Rich does a high dive. All swim. We climb from ledge to ledge, from fall to fall, up pitches of some difficulty. The seven hairy boatmen are there, everywhere, grinning like Bushmen, always ready with a helping hand on wrist, on arm, on thigh or buttock—wherever needed. "A boatman's work is never done," explains Wally, boosting Salome in her mini-bikini up into a rock chimney, where Sharky waits above, teeth gleaming.

We watch the boatmen traverse one ledge with a rather indecent exposure, two hundred feet of vertical space full of nothing but gravity. The ledge is three inches wide. There are no handholds. Most of us choose the sole alternate route, a humiliating crawl on face and belly through a claustrophobic tunnel. No matter. More wonders wait beyond. The route terminates in a kind of amphitheater deep in the cliffs, where warblers sing in the redbud trees and a whispering, shimmering, vaporous veil of crystalline water slips down and down, over moss and algae, past maidenhair fern and helleborine orchid, from the notch in the canyon far above our heads. A breeze caresses the leaves of the willows, hackberrys, box elders. Meditation time.

DAY 9 Drifting down the river after lunch. Riding in Dane's boat now. Sun shimmering in the cloudless sky like a struck and brassy gong. Great balls of fire! and clash of silent symbols. One of the passengers suggests a water fight with the next dory. Dane shudders. "Please," he says, "I hate to get wet. I hate water."

What's this? A boatman who hates to get wet? hates water? Of course. Would you trust a boatman who *likes* water? Beware of lean cooks—and wet boatmen.

Onward and downward. Today we run Forster Rapid (promptly renamed Old Forster) and Fossil Rapid (facile). Then through Specter Rapid, well named for its sinister looming rocks, and Bedrock and Dubendorff. The water is low and the boatmen are concerned about the rocks and waves. There is much going ashore for study, shaking of heads, pointing of hands, debate and council. Like most of the other passengers, I don't understand their technical problems and spend most of my time gazing longingly up the side canyons toward the mysteries of the real wilderness.

Late in the day we land at the mouth of Tapeats Creek, Mile 134. A gravel bar in the middle of the creek prevents us from reaching the campsite on the downriver side of the creek. Because the water between the gravel bar and campsite is shallow enough, we are able to leave the boats on the bar and carry our supplies across the waist-deep water.

DAY **10** Today we hike up Tapeats Canyon and visit one of its tributaries, Thunder River, a great gush of frothy water pouring from a cave in the Redwall. The Redwall limestone formation is full of caverns, partially explored. The whole Kaibab Plateau is full of holes, of which Grand Canyon happens to be merely the most conspicuous.

Half a dozen young nudists from Oakland are camped at Thunder River. The area below the spring looks like it's been trampled by horses. Scarcely a blade of grass or a square foot of undisturbed soil remains. But it wasn't horses. It was people.

All the same, Thunder River is a delightful place. I remember the time a friend and I walked down here from the North Rim, twenty miles in the desert heat of August. Parched as skeletons, we trudged through the heat waves of Surprise Valley (surprise! no shade at all), topped out on a saddle, and looking down, saw these roaring springs, those cool green cottonwood trees, in the middle of the red inferno. Paradise. Of course we'd heard it was here—but we didn't *know* it was here.

A pretty little black and white snake with a white spot on the top of its head, like a caste mark, like a tiny crown, slips across the trail. King snake. It hides deep in the shade of the rocks.

Late in the evening, returning, Renée and I pause on the rim trail high above the mouth of Tapeats Creek and look down at our camp. Shady twilight down in there. Moon rising to the east. Some of the girls are shampooing their hair in the river. Wally and Dane are casting for trout in the creek. Smoke rises slowly, a casual pillar of blue, from the fire. Jenny and Kenly are making a salad. Others lie about reading, dozing, talking, sipping drinks. Murmur of voices. People. Humans more or less, like us, enjoying the ease of a perfect evening, the beauty of a splendid place. And we hear Sharky and Rich with their recorders, playing a duet; the melody of an old, old Shaker hymn floats up toward us on the quiet air:

> *Tis a gift to be simple*
> *Tis a gift to be free*
> *Tis a gift to come down*
> *Where you ought to be. . . .*

DAY **11** The river bears us on. We are leaving Granite Narrows, its tranquil waters, its polished and tortured, embittered and sculpted antique diamond-hard scratch-proof Archean schist. Yes, I'm thinking, it's true, ancient rocks, like old folks, acquire character through endurance of time and adversity, acquire beauty through character. Heraclitus, another riverman, took the words out of my mouth two thousand years ago—"A man's fate is his character. His character is his fate."

Now what? We've run all the really big rapids except the riffle at Mile 179, we've lost nary a soul, we've salvaged several cans of Coors from Beerdrop Falls, we've done Middle Granite Gorge and Thunder River and Deer Creek Falls—

> *August 23, 1869—Just after dinner we pass a stream on the right, which leaps into the Colorado by a direct fall of more than 100 feet, forming a beautiful cascade. On the rocks in the cavelike chamber are ferns, with delicate fronds and enameled stalks. . . .*

Right. At Mile 144, dropping down through Kanab Rapid (2–5), we see a bighorn ram on the left bank. Alone, he paces up and down in a state of mild agitation, as if guarding something, or awaiting somebody. Magnificent beast, proud, erect, alert, bright-eyed, with a full curl to his horns. What a nice trophy his head would make on your rumpus-room wall, oh Mr. Grand-Slammer, you twinkly-eyed mischievous fellow, with your scope-sighted Weatherby 30.06. How about *your* head, properly cleaned and stewed and stuffed, of course, mounted on the canyon wall?

Four miles farther and half a mile up Matkatamiba Canyon one of our party spots more sheep, a half-dozen ewes. Maybe that's what the big fellow was anxious about. We've invaded his turf.

DAY **12** Onward, quickly. Through treacherous Upset Rapid (3–8) where Shorty Burton died, back in '67. We doff headgear in his memory. Going around the bend. Views of Mount Sinyala, above Havasupai country, where the Supai Indians, a small tribe, make their home. The river turns south, west, north, west, and southwest, every which way but loose. We pause for half a day at Havasu Creek.

Blue water, full of travertine. This limestone solution tends to form hard, stony barriers, like little dams, as it flows down the creek to the river. As a result Havasu Creek consists of many falls, cascades, and pools. The pools are deep, clear, and blue as the swimming pools of Phoenix. The falls come in many sizes, including the 200-foot plunge of Mooney Falls, seven miles upstream from the river.

DAY **13** In the morning the river is low. John looks grim. I check the rock. High and dry, and the river dropping slowly.

Breakfast is finished. We load the dories. Some of the boatmen are concerned that their boats are too light, since most of the food is gone. They place large rocks in the bottom of the hatches for ballast. The extra weight down low may help at Mile 179.

> *August 13, 1869—What falls there are, we know not; what rocks beset the channel, we know not; what walls rise over the river, we know not. . . . The men talk as cheerfully as ever; jests are bandied about freely this morning; but to me the cheer is somber and the jests are ghastly.*

Write on, good Major Powell. How prescient you were. I know exactly how you felt. I can read your every emotion on the face of John Blaustein.

We push off. Sunlight sparkles on the laughing wavelets of the master stream. Little birds twitter in the tamarisk.

It looks like a good day to die. All days are good but this one looks better than most.

80

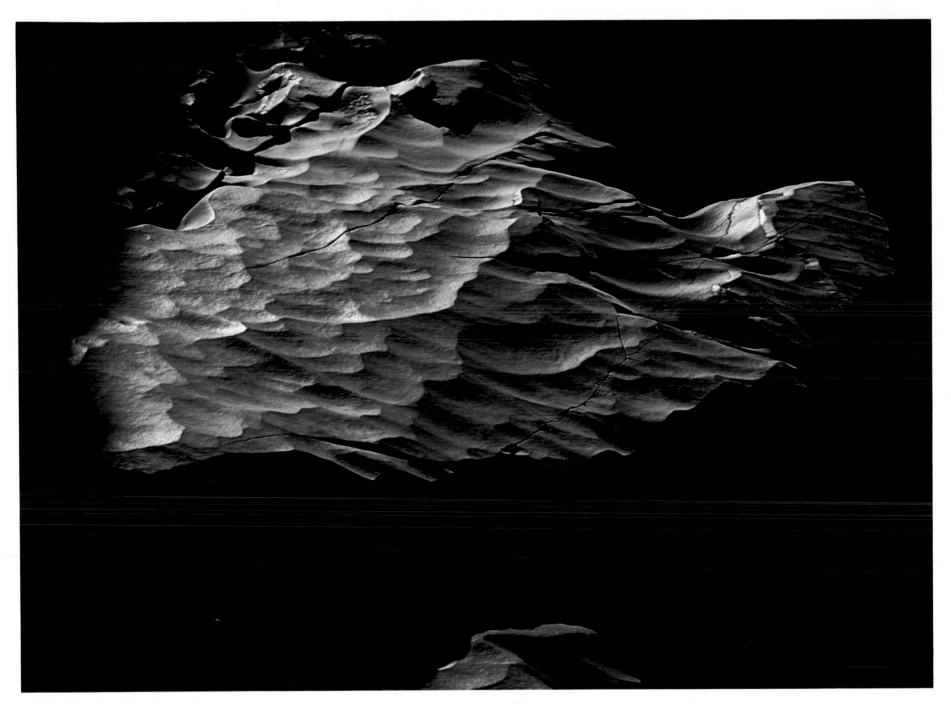